Life Around the World

What's Food Like Around the World?

By Kathleen Connors

New York

Published in 2022 by Cavendish Square Publishing, LLC
243 5th Avenue, Suite 136, New York, NY 10016

First Edition

Library of Congress Cataloging-in-Publication Data
Names: Connors, Kathleen, author.
Title: What's food like around the world? / Kathleen Connors.
Description: First edition. | New York : Cavendish Square Publishing, [2022] | Series: Life around the world | Includes index.
Identifiers: LCCN 2020031843 | ISBN 9781502659446 (library binding) | ISBN 9781502659422 (paperback) | ISBN 9781502659439 (set) | ISBN 9781502659453 (ebook)
Subjects: LCSH: Food–Juvenile literature. | Food habits–Juvenile literature.
Classification: LCC TX355 .C715 2022 | DDC 394.1/2–dc23
LC record available at https://lccn.loc.gov/2020031843

Editor: Kristen Nelson
Designer: Tanya Dellaccio

The photographs in this book are used by permission and through the courtesy of: Cover Tapati Rinchumrus/Shutterstock.com; p. 5 Jose Luis Pelaez Inc/DigitalVision/Getty Images; p. 7 Anjelika Gretskaia/Moment/Getty Images; pp. 9, 21 bhofack2/iStock/Getty Images Plus/Getty Images; p. 11 AlexPro9500/iStock/Getty Images Plus/Getty Images; p. 13 paylessimages/iStock/Getty Images Plus/Getty Images; p. 15 Nico De Pasquale Photography/Moment/Shutterstock.com; p. 17 Photograph by Eric Isaac/Moment Open/Getty Images; p. 19 Teenoo/iStock/Getty Images Plus/Getty Images; p. 23 Frank Rothe/The Image Bank/Getty Images.

Printed in the United States of America

CONTENTS

Food Is Culture

Food is an important part of **culture**. The foods eaten in different parts of the world often have to do with what's grown there. They're also tied to a country's past. What do people around the world eat today?

What Makes a Meal?

In Poland, many meals include dumplings called pierogi. They're often filled with mashed potatoes and then **boiled**. They're sometimes fried too. They can also have other fillings, such as cheese.

Falafel is a meal common in Israel. Chickpeas are ground up, mixed with spices, and fried in a ball. Many people like to eat falafel in a flat bread called pita with cucumber, yogurt, and tomatoes.

In Germany, a meal isn't a meal without sausage! Bratwurst is one of the most **popular** sausages. There are many kinds of bratwurst that all taste a little different. Some are spicy, or hot. Some are sweeter!

Rice is a big part of meals in Japan. Even the smallest children eat rice! With their rice, families may eat fish or tofu. Tofu is made from soybeans. It takes on the taste of what it's cooked with.

In Italy, meals may have **courses**. One course is commonly a kind of pasta. Pasta in Italy doesn't often come from a box! It's made by hand. Pasta is made of just flour, eggs, oil, and salt.

Not So Different

It's common in many places to have bread as part of a meal. That bread is different around the world! In Ethiopia, injera is a flat, or thin, bread made with a tiny **grain** called teff. People use it to scoop up their food.

Naan is a flat bread made in India and other parts of South Asia. It's cooked in a clay oven called a tandoor. Like injera, naan can be used to scoop up food.

What do you put on your sandwich? In Australia, many families like to eat a salty spread called vegemite. Sometimes they add cheese too. Marmite is a spread eaten in South Africa that's much like vegemite.

No matter where you live, it's common to have something sweet at the end of a meal. In Australia, children like to eat sultanas, which are a kind of raisin. Families around the world love ice cream!

WORDS TO KNOW

boiled: Cooked in water that is so hot bubbles rise to the top.

courses: Parts of a meal that are served separately from other parts.

culture: The beliefs and ways of life of a certain group of people.

grain: A seed of a plant used for food.

popular: Liked by many people.

INDEX